Lynn Huggins-Cooper

Contents

CW00956393

Introduction		2
Reading	• **Parent pages**	4
	Reading with your child	4
	Questions to ask when reading with your child	5
	Books chosen for the Reading Test	6
	Books in school	7
Activities	1 About books finding information on the covers	8
	2 Make a library at home! grouping similar books together	9
	3 Can you tell a story? sequencing events	10
	4 Make a puppet show re-telling a story in order	11
	5 Book review bugs! giving an opinion	12
	6 Word bubbles choosing interesting vocabularly	13
	7 Looking at characters describing a person and giving reasons	14
	8 Make your own book writing fiction or non-fiction	15
Comprehension	• **Parent pages**	16
	Consonant and vowel blends	16
	Word bundles	17
Activities	9 Sound flowers learning consonant blends	18
	10 Sound balloons learning vowel sounds in words	19
	11 Scanning looking for key words	20
	12 Reading comprehension: Level 2 example answers to questions on a fiction passage	21
	13 Test yourself: Test 1	22
	14 Reading comprehension: Level 2 example answers to questions on a non-fiction passage	23
	15 Test yourself: Test 2	24
Extension to Level 3	16 Reading comprehension: Level 3 example answers to questions on a non-fiction passage	25
	17 Test yourself: Test 3	26
	18 Test yourself: Test 4	28
	Booklist	30
	Glossary	31
	Answers	32

Introduction

Key Stage 1 National Tests

Children between the ages of 5 and 7 (Years 1 and 2) study Key Stage 1 of the National Curriculum. Between January and June of their final year in Key Stage 1 (Year 2) all children take written National Tests (commonly known as SATs) in English and Mathematics. For the English SAT they also take part in tasks which are assessed as part of their classroom work. The tests and tasks are administered and marked by teachers in school. The test papers are also externally moderated to make sure that they are assessed consistently.

The results of the tasks and tests will be reported to you in July. They will indicate what your child has learned during Key Stage 1, helping you and your child's teacher to assess whether your child is reaching the national standards set out by the National Curriculum.

Understanding your child's level of achievement

The National Curriculum divides standards of performance in each subject into a number of levels, from 1 to 8. On average, children are expected to advance one level for every two years they are at school. By the end of Key Stage 1 (Year 2), your child should be at Level 2. If your child is working at Level 1, there will be some areas of English that they need help with. If your child is working at Level 3, they are doing very well, and are exceeding the targets for their age group. The table shows how your child should progress through the levels at ages 7, 11 and 14 (the end of Key Stages 1, 2 and 3).

Legend:
- ☐ Exceptional performance
- ■ Exceeded targets for age group
- ☐ Achieved targets for age group
- ▦ Working towards targets for age group

	7 years	11 years	14 years
level 8+			☐
level 8			■
level 7			■
level 6		☐	☐
level 5		■	☐
level 4	☐	☐	▦
level 3	■	▦	▦
level 2	☐	▦	▦
level 1	▦	▦	▦

The Tests in English

The National Curriculum divides English into three areas or Attainment Targets. These are 'Speaking and Listening', which is assessed in the course of classroom work, 'Writing', and 'Reading', for which there are written tests.

The Reading Test

Section A: Task, conducted by the teacher

1. An introductory session to discuss a specific book.
2. A general reading test.
3. The child's response to the book, perhaps prompted by verbal questions.

Section B: Written comprehension test

Children read two passages, one-fiction, the other non fiction, and write answers in the test booklet.

Extension to Level 3

Your child's teacher will assess the level at which your child should be tested based on observations made during their time in Key Stage 1. The Level 3 test will be taken by children who are managing Level 2 work with confidence. Most children are expected to achieve Level 2, and it would be sensible to work through the main body of this book before attempting the rather demanding Level 3 comprehension activities on pages 25 to 29.

The test at Level 3 is entirely in the form of written answers to comprehension passages. It has three parts:

1. A story: children write answers to questions in a test booklet.
2. A set of instructions for making something: children answer questions about the instructions.
3. Three contrasting information passages: children compare and contrast different texts.

How this book will help

- This book offers a variety of activities designed to practise the skills your child will need to tackle the Reading Test with confidence.
- This book revises work your child should be doing in class. It does not attempt to teach new material from scratch.
- The *Parent pages* and *Notes to parents,* featured on the children's pages, offer advice to enable you to work with your child, helping to improve skills.
- Activities in this book are designed to promote your child's familiarity with the 'literary language' needed for discussing books, to enhance your child's ability to 'respond to books' in an informed manner, and to enable you to 'listen actively' to your child's reading as teachers do in school.
- The *Test yourself* pages allow your child informal practice for the kinds of tasks and tests including in the National Tests.
- Answers are provided on page 32 to enable your child to learn from mistakes.

Using this book

When helping your child, remember the 'little and often' rule! Children working in Key Stage 1 are still quite young and may be tired after a demanding day at school. Make sure that the atmosphere is relaxed when you carry out the activities, and be ready to stop when you feel your child is becoming tired or frustrated. Above all, the activities in this book have been designed to provide a fun way of learning the skills and knowledge necessary for your child to produce the best possible work in the National Tests.

Reading with your child

Reading partners

Reading with your child is more than just your child reading, and you supplying 'difficult' words when your child is 'stuck'. It is also more than you reading to your child, even though this is a valuable part of all children's 'reading diet', which can continue with proficient readers. Reading together should be an enjoyable partnership between you and your child and it is important to choose a time for it when both of you are relaxed and comfortable. A successful method of reading together, which can avoid the less confident reader becoming tired or frustrated, is to be 'reading partners'. You can either read alternate pages, or you can read a page, then let your child read it again as a type of 'apprenticeship'.

Starting a book

• When your child is ready to start a new book, look at it first yourself, so you have some idea of what to point out or appropriate questions to ask if your child needs prompting.

• Begin your reading session by talking about the book generally. Refer to page 8 and familiarise your child with 'literary language' that may be useful in the discussion.

• Look at the cover together and ask questions about it.
  Does it make your child want to open the book? Why?
  Why did your child choose to read this particular book?

This is how your child's teacher will begin reading sessions in the classroom, and this pattern is used to assess your child for the Key Stage 1 SATs.

Strategies

If 'stuck' on a word, let your child try, but not struggle and become frustrated.
Help to decode words using these strategies:

• Break the words into 'sounds', but not individual letter sounds. For example, caterpillar is sounded out as cat – er – pill – ar.
• Encourage your child to use the words in the rest of the sentence as a clue to help recognise an unfamiliar word.
• Pictures in the book can also give your child clues to help read new words, and this is a strategy that your child's teacher will encourage.

Questions to ask when reading with your child

Developing response skills

When reading with your child, stop at intervals to ask questions. This checks for understanding, and will help your child to respond to literature in an informed manner. The questions should be mainly 'open ended' questions with no 'correct' answers; rather, they should ask for your child's opinion. Similar questions will be asked by your child's teacher during the SATs assessment.

Encourage your child to give 'evidence' for answers by referring back to the text, and to discuss illustrations. Using pictorial information is an important skill in children of this age, and 'reading' the picture helps the child to understand the meaning of the text.

Pick appropriate questions for different books from the list below. Ask your child specific questions about particular books that you think of as you are reading. Let your child maintain the 'flow' of reading, and ask questions at natural pauses, such as the end of a page, chapter or conversation between characters.

Suggested pre-reading questions

Who is your favourite author?
Do you know any other books by the author of the book you are reading?
Do you know of any other books illustrated by the same artist?
What do you think the book is about? What gave you any clues?

Suggested questions for natural pauses

Why do you think ... happened?
Why do you think he/she acted like that?
What do you think ... means?
What do you think will happen next?

Suggested questions to ask after reading

How do you think he/she felt when ... happened?
Can you find words to describe ...? (Give name of character.)
Do the illustrations in this book tell you anything that the words do not?
What style has the illustrator used? (Talk about watercolours, cartoons, collage, line drawings, pencil sketches.)
Can you think of any other stories like this one?
What style of writing is this? (Talk about poetry, plays, non-fiction, magazine or newspaper reports, comics, etc.)

Books chosen for the Reading Test

Criteria

The books for the Level 2 SATs Reading Test are chosen by the test writers according to the following criteria:

- The books will be interesting, covering subjects that your child will relate to and enjoy.

- They will be appropriate in form and content to the age of your child.

- There will be a clear, understandable story line.

- The characters in the stories will be engaging.

- The story will have a clear message or purpose.

- The language will sound interesting when it is read aloud.

- The language will use repetition effectively to familiarise your child with the vocabulary used.

- The illustrations will be interesting and engaging.

- The books will celebrate the multicultural nature of society.

- The books will not reinforce gender stereotyping.

In preparing for the reading SATs, your child's teacher will select three or four of the recommended books with which your child is not already familiar. Your child will then choose independently which of the selected books to read.

Reading at home

When you are choosing books to read at home, bear in mind the criteria on this page. In addition, look at the range of books your child is given to read at school. These are explained on the following page.

Books in school

The range of books

Under National Curriculum guidelines, your child is offered a wide variety of reading materials at school. These include:

Picture books: there is no text and the reader invents a story to accompany the illustrations. This enables the reader to compose stories in their own words. It also allows the 'listener' to assess the reader's knowledge of 'story language'.

Myths and legends: tales from ancient cultures, such as Greece, Egypt and Rome.

Poetry: an invaluable tool in language development which can teach about rhyme and descriptive language such as similes and metaphors; it also supports the development of 'Speaking and Listening' skills when used for dramatic reading and discussions.

Plays: in simple forms, these promote paired and group reading and support the development of skills in 'Speaking and Listening'.

Traditional tales from different cultures: certain stories such as Cinderella occur in many cultures and demonstrate cultural commonality in the world. They tend to follow familiar patterns, but the cultural differences make them new and interesting.

Contemporary children's books: including simple short story collections.

Classic children's literature: this section is for the more confident reader. The texts can be quite complex, but story tapes, or sections of the books read aloud by parents, can be a useful introduction.

Good quality non-fiction books: with clear text and illustrations which introduce your child to tools such as an index, a contents page, and a glossary.

Magazines, comics and newspaper articles: these are chosen to suit the age and ability of the children.

Finding books yourself

When you are choosing books to read at home, it would be useful to reflect the variety that your child meets in school.

Most bookshops have comfortable children's sections, where your child can 'try before you buy'. There are also many good quality book clubs which expressly cater for children and their parents: your child's school may run one. Libraries often run story reading sessions and themed activity days. All of these book sources are aware of the requirements of the National Curriculum.

 **About books**

Can you talk about books? Look at the picture:

back cover　　**spine**　　**front cover**

Selina and the Sleepy Dragon

One night, Selina finds a large scaly dragon asleep in her bed! When she wakes him up he smiles, yawns and blows smoke in her face. Then he shuts his eyes and starts snoring again. Selina is not pleased! How can she get rid of this sleepy dragon?

ISBN 1-23456-543-2

Mona Seefa **Selina and the Sleepy Dragon** CHILDREN'S PRESS

Selina and the Sleepy Dragon

by Mona Seefa

 CHILDREN'S PRESS

Illustrated by Henry Sparks

title
what the book is called

Mona Seefa has written many books for children. She began writing stories when she was growing up in Egypt, and her first book, *Selina and the Magic Carpet*, won the **Imagine! Children's Book Award**. She now lives in England, and her stories are inspired by well-known fairy story characters – but with a difference!

'blurb'
tells you about the book and helps you decide if you want to read it.

ISBN
this number is the book's 'fingerprint'. Shops use it to find and order books.

bar code
is 'read' by the till in the shop. It 'tells' the till which book has been sold.

publisher's logo
tells you who published the book.

author
who wrote the book.

illustrator
who drew the pictures.

Sometimes you will find a **pen portrait** inside the front or back cover. This is a piece of writing about the author or illustrator.

2 Make a library at home!

Use your own books to play libraries.

| Fiction | Non-fiction | Get your book stamped here! |

Make some labels to show people where things are. Can you think of any other labels you might need?

Make some book displays

Use some non-fiction books. These are books with information in them. Put your books about animals together with a sign saying 'Animal books'. Put soft toys or farm and zoo animals near the books.

Make a display of fiction books. This means stories, poems and plays. Put some story books together with a sign that asks 'Do you like stories?' Can you think of more questions to add to the sign?

Choose a favourite story book for a special display. For *Dinosaurs and All That Rubbish* by Michael Foreman you could put out some toy dinosaurs.

When you are ready, all you need are some 'customers'. Ask your friends and family to come and see your very own library!

Tip for parents

Next time you visit the library, discuss what you see with your child. Encourage your child to get ideas for displays, reviews, etc. and to divide books into fiction and non-fiction, like a real library.

Notes to parents

This library role-play will enable your child to be a 'book expert'. When acting as a customer, ask 'the librarian' to recommend a book about animals, sport, holidays – anything that your child will be able to talk about. Encourage your child to use the 'literary language' on page 8. Provide 'props' to make the role-play as engaging as possible – perhaps a cheap stamp and ink pad, and paper to 'stamp' as a book is issued.

③ Can you tell a story?

Do you know the story of *The Three Little Pigs*?

Here are nine sentences from the story.
Can you put them in the right order?
Write the numbers 1 to 9 in the boxes to show the right order.

The wolf huffed and puffed and blew until his face was red, but the pigs were safe and cosy in the house of bricks.	☐
The first pig built his house of straw.	☐
"It's time you had homes of your own!" said Mother Pig.	☐
The first pig ran away to his brother's house made of sticks.	☐
The Big Bad Wolf came and huffed and puffed and the house of straw blew away.	☐
The third pig built his house of bricks.	☐
The Big Bad Wolf came and huffed, and puffed and blew the house of sticks away.	☐
The second pig built his house of sticks.	☐
The first and second pig ran away to their brother's house made of bricks.	☐

Tip for parents

Make sure your child reads all the sentences before attempting to put them in order.

Notes to parents

This activity practises the recall and sequencing of events. Your child will need these skills to describe events in stories accurately and in the correct order. You can give further practice by writing the main events of other well-known stories, such as *Red Riding Hood* or *Cinderella*, on pieces of card. Muddle the cards up and give them to your child to put in sequence.

 **4**

Make a puppet show

Now have some fun!

Make some puppets and put on The Three Little Pigs Show.

You will need:

5 lolly sticks or strips of thick card
a sheet of thin card or thick paper
sticky tape
pens or crayons
safety scissors

1 Copy these shapes onto card.

2 With the help of an adult, cut them out and colour them in.

3 Use tape to stick them to the lolly sticks or card strips.

Now use the puppets you have made to tell the story.

Tip for parents

To extend this activity, help your child to make or find any pieces of scenery that might be needed, and assist with writing a poster advertising the show.

Notes to parents

When your child has performed the story once ask your if you can talk to the characters about what they felt, and why they acted in the way they did during the story. Encourage your child to answer (with the puppets as props) 'in character'. This will help your child to develop skills that are useful for answering questions in a comprehension exercise.

5 Book review bugs!

Maya has written about the books she has read on these book bugs.

Title: The Patchwork Quilt
Author: Valerie Flournoy
Favourite character: Grandma, because she teaches Tanya about keeping memories.
Best part: When the quilt is finished and Grandma is well again.

Title: : Giant
Author: Juliet and Charles Snape
Favourite character: Giant, because she is beautiful and wise.
Best part: When Giant pulls up the river bed and puts out the fire.

Activity

Ask for some paper and invent book bugs of your own! As you finish a book, write about it on the bug.

Write about a book you have read on this bug.

Title:

Author:

Favourite character:

Best part:

Notes to parents

These book bugs are a fun way for your child to record responses to books. Ask your child to tell you about books, concentrating on the reasons for liking or not liking them. Encourage references to the actual text wherever possible. If your child has not enjoyed a book, it is alright to say so, but always ask for reasons. This will help to develop a discerning approach to books.

6 Word bubbles

morning mist

silken

spangled

When you are reading, do you ever find words that you enjoy saying? Poems often have lots of wonderful words and descriptions.

Read the first part of this poem. Jake has read it and he has written his favourite words in the bubbles on the right.

The spider's web, a silken sheet
Hanging across the gate.
Was it there yesterday?
Today, the morning mist
Has spangled it with diamonds.

Jake said, 'I liked 'silken' because it sounds soft and I think a spider's web would feel soft. I liked the way 'morning mist' used the same 'm' sound. 'Spangled' is a new word and I like the way it feels when you say it.'

Now read the second part and choose the words and phrases you like best.

The windfall apple, a red balloon
Laying on the grass.
Was it there yesterday?
Today, the morning frost
Has sprinkled it with glitter.

Activity

Draw your own bubbles on paper. Write in them the words you have chosen. Say why you have chosen them.

Notes to parents

Discuss together you child's choice of words from the poem and the reasons for choosing them. This activity helps your child to form an idea of the kind of language that makes a story or poem interesting. Poetry is an excellent starting point for looking at language, and there are many wonderful collections available (see page 30 for suggested reading). Words learned will also help your child to develop writing skills by using a more varied vocabulary.

7 Looking at characters

Tip for parents

Encourage your child to give reasons for ideas about characters by talking about what they do or say in the story.

Can you describe a character from a book you have just read? Here is Bethany's description of Camille from the book *Camille and the Sunflowers* by Laurence Anholt.

Camille is helpful because he helps his dad collect the mail bags and picked flowers for Vincent.

Camille is imaginative because he dreams about Vincent painting the stars.

Camille is kind because he worried about Vincent and really wants him to stay.

Activity

Now it's your turn to describe a character. You can choose one from your own books, or you can describe a well-known character.

Cinderella
What is she like?
Why do you think so?

Jack
What is he like?
Why do you think so?

Notes to parents

Ask your child to choose a book and read it together. Before your child writes about a character, discuss the story, using some of the questions on page 5. Help by recording what your child says. Often children can discuss complex ideas before they can express them on paper. In the SAT your child's teacher will be looking for good understanding of texts, and the ability to refer back to the story in a verbal discussion.

8 Make your own book

Make your own books to put in your home library. Here are some ideas.

See how I've grown!

For this book you could use a notebook or a scrapbook if you do not want to make the whole book yourself. This is going to be a book about you. It is a non-fiction book because it has facts and information in it.

- Ask for some photographs of yourself as a baby, a toddler, the day you started school and at other events you can remember.
- Stick a photograph on each page and write something about yourself underneath.
- Make a cover and ask for help to fix the pages inside. Write the title of the book and the author – that's you!

Shaped books

When you write a story or an information book, you can make a shaped cover to match your writing.

Here are some ideas:

Ahmed could also use this robot-shaped cover for his information book, *Modern machines.*

Lisa could also use this fish-shaped cover for her story, *The magic fish.*

Tip for parents

A book made at home will have special relevance to your child and increase self-confidence.

Notes to parents

There are more suggestions for ways of making books in *Key Stage 1 Writing*, also in this series. If your child particularly enjoys this activity, a good children's reference library should have craft books which develop these ideas further.

Consonant and vowel blends

'Word attack' skills

Blends are letters which, when written together, make up many of the 'sounds' in the English language. It is better to break words down into component sounds rather than individual letter sounds (see page 18). A knowledge of these blends and the sounds they make will enhance your child's 'word attack' skills – the strategies for 'de-coding' unfamiliar words. Your child's reading will improve as the confidence to tackle unfamiliar words grows.

Activities

Use these activities to help your child to identify consonant and vowel blends (see below).

- Collect newspapers, magazines and junk mail.
- Ask your child to highlight words containing the targeted blend.
- Tear or cut the words out.
- Stick or write the words with consonant blends onto the 'petals' of the sunflower on page 18.
- Stick the words with vowel blends on to the balloon on page 19.

Extension

- Encourage your child to look for the targeted blend in the general environment – at the shops, on notices, in magazines and reading books. This will build an awareness of consonant blends quickly and in an enjoyable manner.
- Make lists of the words that use the targeted blend.
- Point out blends that occur in particular places in words, for example, *lm, nd, ng, nk* at the end of words in English. This will also help spelling skills.

List of suggested blends

Consonant blends

sh, ch, th, ck, bl, st, sp, sk, sm, tw, lk, lm, nd, ng, nk

Vowel blends

ea, ee, oo, oa, ai, oi, ou, ie, ay, oy

Word bundles

Method

This activity will help to increase 'sight vocabulary': words that your child recognises immediately.

You will need:
  black marker
  scissors
  string, elastic or individual ring binders
  card

- Cut out rectangles of card approximately 10 cm by 4 cm.
- Write the chosen words onto the cards.
- Punch a hole at the left-hand edge of the cards.
- Thread them onto the string, elastic or binders in sets of 6 to 8.

Word families and word groups

You can make word bundles for particular groups of words such as the months or days of the week, or you can arrange them in word families (words with the same letter patterns), which are easier to learn as a set, for example:

bell fell sell tell well

You can also make bundles of words your child currently struggles with when you are reading. You could select from this list of common words, picking out those that need practice, or make a bundle for each row and encourage your child to learn one bundle a week.

Common words

had we it so with he and an him the old big we at be was of on

here as you all what new or come get call in which two for do over

with that she down look because they off into this out now up will

went me have can our only would could right make then her but why

been my not if did how where want how there for have one

9 Sound flowers

Read the words on these flowers.

shut shed
shape **sh** shake
shell ship

These words all begin with the sound, **sh**.

chip chat
chick **ch** church
chop chin

These words all begin with the sound, **ch**.

Make your own sound flower.

Notes to parents

Encourage your child to find the targeted blend from different sources: books, magazines, newspapers, signs and notices. Copy the large flower onto coloured paper. Help your child to write the targeted blend on the centre, then to stick or write the words onto the petals. As flowers are filled up, they can be made into a 'consonant blend garden' for the wall. Target one or two blends a week.

10 Sound balloons

Read the words in the balloons.

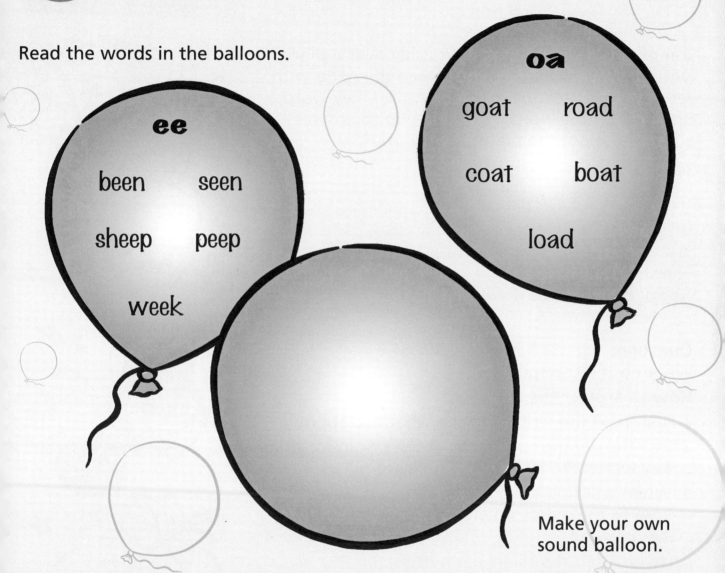

ee

been   seen

sheep   peep

week

oa

goat   road

coat   boat

load

Make your own
sound balloon.

Notes to parents

Use the balloon in the same way as the flower on page 18, targeting one or two vowel sounds a week. Pin filled in balloons on the wall in a bunch for your child to practise reading. The activities on this page assist word recognition and spelling skills.

11 Scanning

Tip for parents

Encourage your child to read the piece of writing several times before attempting to answer the questions.

Scanning is a way of looking quickly over a piece of writing. When you scan, you sweep the page with your eyes like laser beams, looking for 'key words'. Finding the 'key words' will help you to answer questions about the piece of writing.

Read about peacock butterflies.

> Peacock butterflies lay their eggs on nettles. When the caterpillars hatch, they eat the prickly leaves. The butterflies drink nectar from flowers in the garden. They have a tongue like a tube that helps them to suck nectar from deep inside flowers.

Question:
What do the caterpillars eat?

How to answer the question:

1. First, read the writing to see what it is about.
2. Scan the writing to find the answer. Scan for these 'key words' from the question: caterpillars, eat.
3. When you find the 'key words', read the writing close to the words slowly to find the answer to the question.

Answer: The caterpillars eat nettles.

Notes to parents

This activity helps to prepare your child for answering the kind of comprehension questions that appear in the SATs. Reading the piece several times before answering questions should ensure that your child has a good grasp of its content, and will know roughly where to scan to find the key words from the question.

Read about Gracie. Ellie has answered the questions.

Gracie is a goat. She is a kid, which means she is just a baby. Her fur is brown and she has tiny black horns on her head. She likes to eat grass, leaves and dried oats. Gracie sleeps in a stable with her friends, the rabbits. Usually she shares her food with them, but she can be naughty and sometimes climbs into the feed bin and eats the rabbit food! She likes to skip and jump in the fields when it is sunny.

1. What sort of animal is Gracie?
   - ☐ a rabbit   ☐ a cat
   - ☐ a horse   ☑ a goat

2. Gracie is a 'kid.' What does this mean?
   A kid is a baby goat.

3. What colour is Gracie's fur?
   Gracie's fur is brown.

4. What is Gracie's favourite food?
   Gracie likes to eat grass, oats and leaves.

5. Where does Gracie sleep?
   - ☐ in a field   ☐ in the feed bin
   - ☑ in the stable   ☐ under some leaves

Question

Where does Gracie play when it is sunny?

Tip for parents

Make sure your child reads the passage through several times before reading the questions and looking at the answers.

Test 1

Read more about Gracie. Answer the questions.

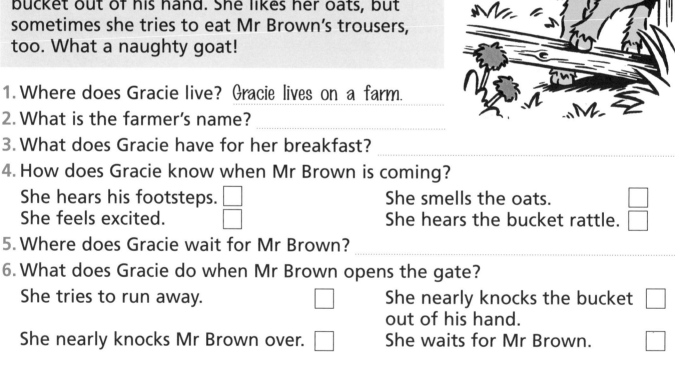

Gracie lives on a farm in the country. The farm belongs to Mr Brown. Every morning he brings Gracie a bucket of oats for her breakfast. When she hears the bucket rattle, she knows he is coming. She runs to the farmyard gate to wait for him. She gets very excited, and when Mr Brown opens the gate she nearly knocks the bucket out of his hand. She likes her oats, but sometimes she tries to eat Mr Brown's trousers, too. What a naughty goat!

1. Where does Gracie live? Gracie lives on a farm.
2. What is the farmer's name? ....
3. What does Gracie have for her breakfast? ....
4. How does Gracie know when Mr Brown is coming?

   She hears his footsteps. ☐   She smells the oats. ☐
   She feels excited. ☐   She hears the bucket rattle. ☐

5. Where does Gracie wait for Mr Brown? ....
6. What does Gracie do when Mr Brown opens the gate?

   She tries to run away. ☐   She nearly knocks the bucket ☐
                                      out of his hand.
   She nearly knocks Mr Brown over. ☐   She waits for Mr Brown. ☐

Read this passage. John has answered the questions.

Have you ever been on holiday?

Some people like to go abroad because they think the weather will be better.

Other people like to stay in England. They might visit London because there are lots of interesting things to do in the capital city. On a hot day they might choose to take a boat trip on the river. When it is raining, they might go to a museum.

For people who like to relax and have fun, the seaside is a good place to go. But if it is wet all the time it can be miserable!

Question

What is the seaside like if it is wet all the time?

1. Why do some people like to go on holiday abroad?
   They think the weather will be better abroad.

2. Why might people visit London?
   Because they are on holiday. ☐ Because there are interesting things to do. ☑
   Because it is the capital city. ☐ Because it won't rain there. ☐

3. What can people do on a rainy day in London?
   They can go to a museum.

4. People go to the seaside to
   relax and have fun ☑   sunbathe ☐
   read books ☐   go swimming ☐

— Notes to parents —

This activity practises scanning for answers to questions about a non-fiction passage. When your child has read the passage several times, and looked at the questions and answers, cover them and ask your child to point to the key words from the questions in the passage.

15 Test 2

Read this passage and answer the questions.

Diwali is the Festival of Lights, and it is celebrated between mid October and mid November by many Hindu and Sikh people all over the world. Houses and shops are cleaned until they sparkle, and doorsteps are decorated with wonderful patterns made from sweet smelling spices and coloured powder. These are called Rangoli patterns. People light beautiful clay lamps called 'diwas'. Everyone wears new clothes and families get together for parties and celebrations, and often give each other presents. Fireworks are sometimes let off to celebrate Diwali.

1. What is the Festival of Lights called?

☐ October ☐ Hindu ☐ Diwali ☐ Diwas

2. What are the patterns made from spice called?

....

3. What are 'diwas'? ....

4. What do people often give each other at Diwali?

☐ new clothes ☐ fireworks

☐ clay lamps ☐ presents

5. Why are fireworks let off?

....

....

....

....

....

....

Notes to parents

This test is designed to practise the skills necessary for your child to answer comprehension questions with confidence. This will help them with their SATs at Key Stage 1, but it will also be of benefit as they move into Key Stage 2 and beyond.

16 Reading comprehension
Level 3

Make a butterfly on a string!

You will need:

paper	stick or twig 30 cm long
sewing thread	sticky tape
scissors	crayons or paper scraps and glue

1. Fold the paper in half and cut out a 'half butterfly' shape.

2. Decorate the butterfly shape.

3. Cut a piece of thread 30 cm long.

4. Tape one end of the thread to the butterfly.

5. Tape the other end of the thread to the stick.

6. You are ready to flap your butterfly. Have fun!

When you have made your butterfly, answer these questions.

Number 1 has been done for you.

1. How did the instructions tell you to make the butterfly shape?

You had to fold the paper and cut out half the shape.

2. How did you attach the thread to the butterfly's head?

3. What did you use the crayons or paper shapes for?

Notes to parents

This exercise is designed to help your child develop the ability to get information from instructions, in the same way as is required by the Level 3 Reading SATs test. To practise this activity, ask similar questions to those on this page when your child is doing art and craft activities at home.

17 Test 3

Read this pizza recipe, then
answer the questions on page 27.

Make pizza faces!

(Serves 4) Ingredients:

4 cheese and tomato pizza bases
100 grams of Red Leicester cheese, grated
4 tablespoons of sweetcorn
1 tomato
8 olives

1. Put two olives on each pizza as 'eyes'.

2. Ask an adult to help you to cut the tomato into four wedges. These will be the 'mouths' for each face.

3. Mix the cheese and the sweetcorn together in a bowl.

4. Sprinkle the mixture around the top edge of each pizza to make 'hair.'

5. Ask an adult to help you to put the pizzas in a warm oven, or under the grill until the cheese bubbles – then you will know your pizzas are ready!

1. Which ingredient in the recipe do you cut with a knife?

   Circle the answer.

   | olives | onion | tomato |

2. Which ingredient is mixed with Red Leicester cheese to make 'hair'?

   ....

3. Which ingredient is used to make the mouths?

   ....

4. How do you know when the pizza is cooked?

   ....

5. Which ingredient do you use to make the eyes?

   ....

6. What shape are the mouths?

   ....

7. How many olives do you need for the recipe?

   ....

Notes to parents

Encourage your child to read a variety of instructions. Recipes are useful, so are instructions for making things in children's activity books. Making things by following instructions will give your child useful practice in scanning the text to find the next step.

18 Test 4

Read the story about Tina, then answer the questions.

Tina's Dream

Tina was cross. Very cross. To prove how cross she was, she stamped on the can she had been kicking along the street. It made a wonderful crunching noise that made her feel a little better, but not much. It wasn't fair – just because she was a girl, Paul and Andrew wouldn't let her play football with them.

Tina climbed up on the wall to think. The shade of the plants from the garden helped her to cool down. She knew she was just as good as the boys, and better than some of them! She wondered to herself if that was the problem. Perhaps they were afraid she would show them up!

Tina leaned back on the cool, smooth wall. She closed her eyes and drifted into her favourite daydream.

She was wearing a white football shirt, and yes, as you got closer you could see it was an England shirt! The crowd were roaring, 'Tina! Tina!' She beat one defender, then another and blasted a shot towards the open goal and 'Yes!' the crowd screamed as the ball flew into the net.

'What are you grinning at, stupid?' said a voice. Tina opened her eyes and smiled. It was her friend Bibby. Tina jumped down from the wall and grabbed her friend. Bibby had a brand new ball with her.

'Present from my Auntie!' she explained. They ran down the road, shouting and kicking the ball backwards and forwards between them. 'One day,' thought Tina to herself.

1. How was Tina feeling at the beginning of the story?

   ....

2. Why was Tina feeling this way?

   ....

3. What did Tina think at first was the reason why the boys would not let her play?

   ....

4. Tina thought the boys were afraid of something. What was it?

   She would be a problem. ☐
   She would show them up. ☐
   She would be much better than them. ☐
   She wouldn't be as good as them. ☐

5. What was Tina's daydream about?

   ....

6. What stopped Tina's daydream?

   ....

7. Where had Bibby got her new ball from?

   ....

Booklist

This is a small selection of books to share with your child. Some will be suitable for your child to read alone; others will better read by you or as a paired reader. The books on this list are favourites in primary schools – with teachers and children!

Frog and Toad are Friends – Arnold Lobel
Piggybook, Gorilla, Willy the Wimp – and any other books by Anthony Browne
Our Cat Flossie – Ruth Brown
The Church Mice series – Graham Oakley
Burglar Bill, Please Mrs Butler, Miss Dose the Doctor's Daughter – and any other
    books by Alan and Janet Ahlberg
The Patchwork Quilt – Valerie Flournoy
Not Now Bernard – David McKee
War and Peas, Dinosaurs and All That Rubbish – and any other books by
    Michael Foreman
Katie Morag – a series of story books – Marie Hedderwick
Dogger – and any other books by Shirley Hughes
Princess Smartypants, The Smelly Book, The Hairy Book – and any other books by
    Babette Cole
Badger's Parting Gifts – Susan Varley
Where The Wild Things Are – Maurice Sendak
The Julian Stories – Anne Cameron
A Necklace of Raindrops – Joan Aitken
How the Whale Became and Other Stories – Ted Hughes
The Selfish Giant – Oscar Wilde and Michael Foreman
Catkin, The Leopard's Drum – Antonia Barber
A is For Africa – Ifeoma Onyefulu
I is For India – Prodeepta Das
Degas and the Little Dancer, Camille and the Sunflowers – Laurence Anholt
The Winter Hedgehog, Norah's Ark – Ann and Reg Cartwright
Dr. Xargle's Book of Earthlets – a series of books by Jeanne Willis and Tony Ross
Nature in Close Up series – non-fiction titles published by A & C Black
Keeping Minibeasts series – Barrie Watts

GLOSSARY

author
(Page 8) a person who writes books

bar code
(Page 8) the lines on the back of a book, 'read' by the shop till

blurb
(Page 8) a short description of what a book is about, usually on the back cover

book review
(Page 12) a piece of writing discussing a book and giving an opinion about it

character
(Page 14) a person in a story

fiction
(Page 9) story books

illustrator
(Page 8) a person who draws pictures for a book

ISBN
(Page 8) the number that identifies a book

non-fiction
(Page 9) information books

pen portrait
(Page 8) a short piece of writing about the author of a book, usually on the back cover or the inside back cover

publisher's logo
(Page 8) the symbol that shows who has published a book: Walker Books have a teddy bear

scanning
(Page 20) looking quickly over a piece of writing to find the key words

title
(Page 8) what a book or story is called

ANSWERS

Answers to questions

Page 7
Can you tell a story?
This is a suggested order. If
you feel your child has chosen a
different order but it still makes
sense, treat it as correct.

Reading the boxes down the page:
9, 2, 1, 6, 5, 4, 7, 3, 8.

Page 21
Gracie likes to play in the fields.

Page 23
It is miserable.

Page 25
2. With sticky tape.
3. Decorating the butterfly.

Answers to tests

Test 1 **Page 22**
1. Gracie lives on a farm.
2. The farmer's name is Mr Brown.
3. Gracie has a bucket of oats for breakfast.
4. She hears the bucket rattle.
5. She waits for Mr Brown by the farmyard gate.
6. She nearly knocks the bucket out of his hand.

Test 2 **Page 24**
1. The Festival of Lights is called Diwali.
2. The patterns made from spice are called Rangoli.
3. Diwas are clay lamps.
4. Presents
5. To celebrate Diwali

Test 3 **Page 26**
1. Tomato
2. Sweetcorn
3. Tomato
4. The cheese bubbles.
5. Olives
6. Wedges
7. Eight

Test 4 **Page 29**
1. Cross
2. The boys would not let her play football with them.
3. Because she was a girl.
4. She would be much better than them.
5. Playing football for England.
6. Tina's friend Bibby spoke to her and stopped her dreaming.
7. From her Auntie.